slices of an
ABUNDANT

slices of an
ABUNDANT
LIFE

Mark Kuraya

TATE PUBLISHING & Enterprises

Slices of an Abundant Life
Copyright © 2011 by Mark Kuraya. All rights reserved.

Scripture quotations marked "NIV" are taken from the *Holy Bible, New International Version* ®, Copyright © 1973, 1978, 1984 by International Bible Society. Used by permission of Zondervan Publishing House. All rights reserved.

Scripture quotations taken from the *New American Standard Bible*®, Copyright © 1960, 1962, 1963, 1968, 1971, 1972, 1973, 1975, 1977, 1995 by The Lockman Foundation. Used by permission.

Scripture taken from the *New King James Version*®. Copyright © 1982 by Thomas Nelson, Inc. Used by permission. All rights reserved.

The opinions expressed by the author are not necessarily those of Tate Publishing, LLC.

Published by Tate Publishing & Enterprises, LLC
127 E. Trade Center Terrace | Mustang, Oklahoma 73064 USA
1.888.361.9473 | www.tatepublishing.com

Tate Publishing is committed to excellence in the publishing industry. The company reflects the philosophy established by the founders, based on Psalm 68:11,
"The Lord gave the word and great was the company of those who published it."

Book design copyright © 2011 by Tate Publishing, LLC. All rights reserved.
Cover design by Kristen Verser
Interior design by Leah LeFlore

Published in the United States of America

ISBN: 978-1-61777-205-4
1. Self-Help, Motivational & Inspirational
2. Religion, Christian Life, Inspirational
11.02.24

DEDICATION

To God be the glory, great things he hath done!

I give God all the praise and glory for all he has given and has allowed me to accomplish. Years ago, he honored a desperate prayer of a sinful and broken man. I would also like to dedicate this book to my parents, Ben and Ayako Kuraya, who demonstrated by their own lives how to live courageously and sacrificially. My deepest gratitude and respect for them will always be part of my memory and how God provided so well and perfectly for me in them.

—Mark N. Kuraya 2010

ACKNOWLEDGMENTS

My family: Lila and Bobby; Mom and Dad; Sue and Russell, Noel, Karen, David, Ann, and Brad. David and Jan Anzai and Family. Aidyn and Jayda The Gushikumis: Mike, Sue, David, and Sarah; Colin, Eugenie, Cecily, Brian, and Jonathan; Carlton, Keiko, Andrew, and Kacie. Pastors Nelson Kwon, Howard Yoshida, Ted Ogoshi, Don Asman, Gerald Chinen, Wayne Ibara, Randy Furushima, and especially Pastor Michael Angevine. Doctors Raymond Taniguchi, Takanori Fukushima, Sharon Lawler and Kentaro Nishino. My friends at end of the hall: Jimmy and June, Dan and Carol, Bernie and Lori, Terry, Isa, Al and Gloria, and Kelvin Tamura. Special thanks and love to Susan and Dennis Nakaishi, who have helped make so many of my dreams a reality.

TABLE OF CONTENTS

FOREWORD

From Moses to Paul, the Bible gives us a rich and faithful account of people whose lives have been changed because of a personal encounter with the living God. Though no two encounters were alike, when God revealed himself to them, their responses radically and dramatically altered their priorities and changed their lives. As they made themselves available to be used of God, he was able to work his will in and through them to accomplish his purposes to his glory. The call on our lives some two thousand years later is no different.

Each of us has a unique "one-of-a-kind" story through which the Lord continues to reveal himself. Sharing our life experiences and faith-journey stories can serve to encourage others as we come to realize God's faithfulness to us through them. Like the potter working with a lump of clay, God's hands lovingly mold us into the kind of vessel he can use to do his work and will.

So it has been in the life of Mark N. Kuraya. In this collection of personal reflections, Mark shares with us what God has spoken into his heart and has taught him and how each encounter drew him into a closer relationship with the Lord. These sixteen "stories" from Mark's life are about God's goodness and faithfulness to him through the years and the hope he has because of what God has done for him through Jesus Christ. Through each story, God helped to shape his priorities, perspectives, and faith.

Mark has become a precious brother in Christ through the years that we served the Lord through the worship and music ministries at Makiki Christian Church. As we served, we experienced the joy of how God uses "yes" hearts to his glory. However, serving the Lord with his musical gifts was probably not Mark's intention when he first graduated with his Master's in music performance from Indiana University. A gifted musician, he had studied and prepared himself to play professionally with a symphony orchestra. Though he played with the Honolulu Symphony "on call" and was good enough to play in a wide range of gigs (Charo, Gabe Balthazar, Billy Kaui), God closed many doors and, in his time, opened others all the while guiding and directing Mark's path to the church.

As a former orchestra teacher, Mark knew the importance of having a teachable heart. As he made himself more and more available to be used of God, he found himself serving him in ways that he never imagined. Mark brought his gifts and broad range of experiences gained in the music marketplace and applied them to direct the choirs of

Nuuanu Congregational Church and Makiki Christian Church (chancel choir, chamber choir, and family choir) and taught them how to praise the Lord like never before! Oh, the stories he would tell to help the choir better understand the sound or phrasing he knew they could deliver! He helped them to embrace God's call on their lives, to serve him with their voices, and to live lives of worship and praise as a witness through their ministry of music.

In spite of physical limitations and endurance challenges brought on by a series of medical conditions leading to his retirement from the church, with the love and support of his wife, Lila; son, Bobby; and his family and friends, he desires to serve the Lord with his musical gifts.

Mark's life continues to be a work in progress. God is faithful, and Mark knows and trusts that the Lord can still use him, even though he's on permanent disability for medical reasons. Wherever this is, whenever God calls, it is my prayer that Mark's "yes" heart will continue to serve our Savior with the same kind of courage and faith that he has displayed through the challenges of his life. It is a life that has come to know and serve a good and loving God.

—Susan Nakaishi, 2010

REDISCOVERING THE
HEART OF WORSHIP

Shout for joy to the LORD, all the earth. Worship theLORD
with gladness; come before him with joyful songs. Know
that the LORD is God. It is he who made us, and we are
his; we are his people, the sheep of his pasture. Enter his
gates with thanksgiving and his courts with praise; give
thanks to him and praise his name. For the LORD is good
and his love endures forever; his faithfulness continues
through all generations.

Psalm 100:1–5

A s minister of music, I can get so busy in the prepa-
ration of the worship service that I find myself, in
the end, unable to worship. Often enough, my mind
wanders to all the moving parts of the service as I think
about the setting up of the PA system, choosing and sup-
plying the worship musicians with the right music for that
service, being involved in the special music, conducting
the choir, thinking about what songs I would lead during the evening worship, and thinking about all the things

involved for the services next week. Like you, I enjoy and deeply desire to worship God with my brothers and sisters in Christ but feel unable to many times because of what I perceived to be a mountain of distractions. In those times, I feel spiritually robbed and poverty-stricken. It had gotten to a point in 1990 when I felt like I had lost the desire and ability to worship. But God, in his mercy, saw my need.

In the summer of 1990, I attended my first Dimensions in Church Music Conference at Mount Hermon in Santa Cruz, California. One of the highlights of the week was the all-conference Communion service, which took place on Friday. I was in the worship class taught by Doug Lawrence, and we were in charge of planning and implementing this service. When Doug asked for a volunteer to read a scripture, I tried so hard to shrink and pretend I was uninterested. But Doug called my name anyway. *Ugh*! *Why me*? I moaned inwardly. I was torn by feelings of fear and frustration. I didn't want to be put in front of the entire conference during this most special time, and most of all, I just didn't want to do it. But I had to. So I practiced reading the assigned scripture passage over and over and over again the rest of the afternoon, trying to get it just right. It was just like being at home and worrying about the moving parts of the service! I began to dread this service.

But as I sat in the front row, nervously waiting for the service to begin, God opened my eyes and heart in a most special way. I saw members of the faculty sitting and gathered on one side of the room. They were to be our Communion servers. I was deeply touched that these people, who were so distinguished in their field, would be servants to us and to God. I felt so foolish to be so self-conscious and nervous because I had been asked to read a couple of lines of scripture. My eyes were opened to see the big picture of what this service was all about. It wasn't about me (obvious in hindsight). It was about the loving God, who cared enough to reach for me, teach me, and reveal himself to me once again. God revealed to me the heart of worship he had planted in me. It was a really emotional time for me. I will never forget the tears I shed in joy and thanksgiving to God. Nor will I will ever forget the gentle and smiling faces of our faculty as they served the bread and cup to us. They served with such humility and joy, and that was a tremendous witness to me.

> For the LORD takes delight in his people; he crowns the humble with salvation. Let the saints rejoice in this honor and sing for joy on their beds.

> Psalm 149:4–5

I have been given the honor and privilege of worshiping God. It is not something I have attained for myself, but it has been given through the grace of God. No matter what "baggage" I carry during the week, I am still called to worship God. Worship is *not* a thing but an action; it is a "do" word. It is something I am called to do and not just merely prepare or attend. All that I am and all that I have are through the grace of God. I am encouraged to search my heart for the thanks that is owed to God alone. I can remember the words of Josh McDowell when he said that prayer is not dependent on the position of the body but the position of the heart. I think that can be said of worship too. No one can prejudge a person's attitude of worship by how that person looks. God seeks to constantly change the attitude of our hearts and fill it with the desire to praise and worship him. When I turn to him and receive him, I can bow before him in humble joy, praise, and thanks.

If it's been some time since you've heard the still, small voice of God, ask the Good Shepherd to lead you to His pastures beside the still waters where spending time with Him will restore your soul and renew your first love.

SEARCHING FOR THE SOVEREIGN GOD

I am God, and there is no other; I am God, and there is no one like Me, My purpose will be established, and I will accomplish all My good pleasure.

Isaiah 46:9–10

S ince my first aneurysm surgery in 1984, I have been physically and spiritually challenged. In 1994, I spent seven weeks in the hospital following a mild stroke, cardiac arrest, and the discovery of a second aneurysm in my brain. In 1995, arrangements were made for me to go to Allegheny General Hospital in Pittsburgh to have a surgical procedure performed to clip the aneurysm located in a very difficult area of the brain to access. Then, in 1997, a tumor on my brain stem (that appeared in a scan back in 1994 but noted to be the slow-growing type) required me to return to Pittsburgh yet again. For reasons unknown, this tumor had grown to be quite large in just a couple of years. The surgery to remove this tumor lasted twelve hours. The surgeon informed me he had removed all of it successfully. However, in 2001, I was informed that the latest CT scan revealed that the tumor had begun to grow back. It was growing out of the hypoglossal canal at the base of the skull. Treatment meant that I would have to undergo radiotactic surgery. Though it was considered a noninvasive procedure, it was a very complex one. A highly concentrated beam of radiation would blast the tumor from several different angles, guided by a specialized computer. Though this procedure did not promise to eradicate the tumor, it would severely impede its return.

When I found out about this reoccurrence, I became really depressed and afraid. *Not again!* was my silent first reaction. How could God really love me? How could God really care about me when he is continually putting me in the midst of distress and danger? Fear and doubt overcame like a tidal wave. In a panic, I frantically cried out to God and sent up prayers of desperation, pleading for healing. When I calmed down and could step back a bit, it dawned on me that I had been telling God what to do. Without realizing it, I had been ordering him around. Like Gideon, I didn't know to whom I was speaking. I neglected to acknowledge and remember that he is the Sovereign God, the God Most High. But what does that mean? I had to admit to myself that I had very little head knowledge and almost no heart knowledge of God the Most High. (Even to this day, I still struggle to understand and to believe in God's sovereignty. But I *want* to understand and believe. The prayers and the yearning continue on.)

One of the names the Hebrews had for God was El

Enyon—God Most High. He not only set the universe in motion, but he fulfills his purposes for all of his creation. He made all of us and gave us life, and he is strong and wise enough to touch the individual moments of our days. He is aware and involved enough to help us deal with life right now.

But if I don't believe God is sovereign, if he is not in control, if all things are not under his dominion, then he is *not* the Most High, and I am either in the hands of blind fate, in the hands of man, or in the hands of the devil.

When I believe God's plans for me are better than what I could plan for myself, rather than run away from the path he has set before me, I want to run toward it. I don't want to try to change God's mind—his thoughts are perfect. I want to think his thoughts. I don't want to change God's timing—his timing is perfect. I want the grace to accept his timing. I don't want to change God's plan—his plan is perfect. I want to embrace his plan and see how he is glorified through it. I need to try to think his thoughts, accept his timing and embrace his plan.

Submission to God's sovereignty means bowing the knee, whether or not I understand, whether or not I have it figured out, whether or not I agree. In that submission, I can find the strength and grace to keep going. Perhaps I can even find joy in the journey. Whether in good times or in trial, I must run to my El Enyon, trust in his name, and give thanks. I must bend my knee before the God Most High and learn that his sovereign power toward me means nothing less than perfect love.

Scripture encourages us to trust in the Lord with all our hearts and lean not on our own understanding (Proverbs 3:5). God knows that this is easier to say than to do. In your prayers today, humble yourself and ask God to help you trust Him more. Remember that as we humble ourselves before Him, He is faithful and will lift us up (James 4:10).

EDELWEISS

Edelweiss,
Edelweiss,
Every morning you greet me.
Small and white,
Clean and bright,
You look happy to greet me.
Blossom of snow,
May you bloom and grow,
Bloom and grow forever—
Edelweiss,
Edelweiss,
Bless my homeland forever.

This flower, whose fragrance, tender with sweetness, fills the air,
Dispels with glorious splendor the darkness everywhere.

True man, yet very God, from sin and death he saves us
And lightens every load.
Lo! How A Rose E'er Blooming

A bruised reed he will not break, and a smoldering wick
he will not snuff out.

Isaiah 42:3

O n a Maundy Thursday several years ago, Sojourn, a men's quartet of which I was a member, was setting up to rehearse in our sanctuary at about 5:00 in the afternoon. As microphones and speakers were being set up, Nathan Foo spontaneously started singing "Edelweiss" from the Rogers and Hammerstein musical *The Sound of Music*. As Nathan's voice echoed throughout our sanctuary, it struck me how long it had been since I had heard this simple yet beautiful song and I began to recall how I came to know this song.

When I was in the eighth grade, the Kaimuki Inter-mediate School orchestra took a trip to Kona, Hawaii to perform a number of concerts. One of the pieces we played was "Highlights from the Sound of Music." I remem-bered seeing the movie and understanding how the music all fit in with the story. That moment in the movie where Captain von Trapp, played by Christopher Plummer, first sings "Edelweiss" with a simple guitar accompaniment was a touching moment, as his self-controlled and unyield-ing character became softer and more human. This song is used again near the end of the movie during the song contest to allow the entire family to escape from the Nazis. The captain and Maria lead the audience in the singing of the song in a moving display of love and patriotism for their homeland, which was on the verge of Nazi domination.

The lyrics of the song affected me in a different way now as I remembered them. The image of this delicate flower blooming and growing during winter reminded me of the hymn "Lo! How a Rose E're Blooming." The parallel between the flower that was happy to greet you every morning and how Lamentations states that God's mercies are new every morning also struck me. The purity of the blossom and the purity of Christ. The lyrics of the song ask if this flower will bloom and grow forever. Is this not the same desire we have of our life in Christ—that he bloom and grow forever in our lives? Edelweiss blesses its homeland forever. We pray for Christ's blessings and that we may be a blessing to others.

In the midst of all the physical and emotional challenges I've been through I've often felt like the flowers on the hillsides of Austria that endeavor to grow and bloom after a long and cold winter. It's not uncommon for those of us who have traumatic experiences and ongoing struggles, whether they are physical, mental, spiritual or emotional, to forget how to celebrate that the tomb is empty! Christ is alive! I really believe that God is bringing a new spring to us. The winter we have endured is coming to an end. Anyone who has experienced a winter of snow and freezing temperatures knows how much of a joy the coming of spring can bring. The time to thaw ourselves out has come! Let all of us be open to the warmth of his love through his spirit and through his church. Let us ready ourselves for a new beginning. God desires us to bloom and grow and not to wither and die. Praise God for his faithfulness and for his restoration and renewal in us.

God wisely spoke to my heart that day during Sojourn's rehearsal in a way that I could understand him. When Nathan first started singing the song, he couldn't remember the words past the first two lines. As my memory was jarred to remember the lyrics, I really began singing of God's faithfulness. Even when my voice is gone, I hope I never lose the desire to sing to the Lord. Worthy is he of all praise and glory!

WHEN JOY BREAKS THROUGH

"O, Woman," he said, "why are you crying? Who is it you are looking for?" Thinking he was the gardener, she said, "Sir, if you have carried him away, tell me where you have put him, and I will get him." Jesus said to her, "Mary." She turned toward him and cried out in Aramaic, "Rabboni!" (which means teacher). Jesus said, "Do not hold on to me, for I have not yet returned to the Father. Go instead to my brothers and tell them, 'I am returning to my Father and your Father, to my God and your God.'" Mary Magdalene went to the disciples with the news: "I have seen the Lord!"

John 20:15–18

As Easter approaches, I always try to ponder on and remember the miracle of Jesus's resurrection. Sadly, however, though talked about and celebrated year after year, even this miracle of miracles can tend to lose its gravity and true meaning. Like Christmas, it can be just "another season" to get through in the midst of my own busyness, responsibilities, and personal problems. Is it possible to break out and to truly rediscover inwardly and outwardly my joy and thanksgiving for what God has done? How do I understand and then experience this joy?

First, I must always remember that his death and resurrection is truth and not merely a story. The Last Supper, the betrayal, the pain and agony of the cross, and his resurrection are all true. It is not a concoction of a Hollywood screenwriter and special effects crew. This is the work of God. Take the time to reread the story of Christ's passion. Close your eyes and try to imagine what it was like and what Jesus endured for us, the peace and tension of the Last Supper, the despair of the betrayal, the loneliness of Peter as he denied Christ, the agony of the cross, and the utter joy and jubilation of the resurrection. Trying to imagine these feelings and experience these emotions can help to make the gift of the Easter story more personal and become a deeper truth.

I was contemplating Mary's joy as being the first to have seen the risen Lord during one of my devotional studies. At first, she recognizes him as the gardener but then cries out, "Teacher!" That first moment of recognition. That first realization that instantly changes her utter despair to inexplicable joy. What a moment! This sudden and dramatic change reminded me of a series of incidents that occurred while watching the 1992 Winter Olympics.

Probably one of the most glamorous and most popular events in the Winter Olympics is the women's individual figure skating competition. Though I am not a fan of figure skating, I just happened to be watching the 1992 Winter Olympics being held in Albertville just as this event was being telecast. The winning of the gold medal revolved around two women: Kristi Yamaguchi of the United States, and Midori Ito of Japan. My first impression of Midori Ito was how serious she looked. She never smiled, and her face was set and devoid of emotion. She was described as the greatest jumper in the history of women's skating and was favored to win the gold. It turned out, however, that she was not holding up very well under the attention, pressure, and scrutiny of the media and the expectations of her country. Her practice sessions were described by the commentators as shaky and without confidence. In the first round of competition, she fell and missed many of her jumps and failed to even make the top three. Her chance of winning the gold medal was seemingly out of reach. In the days that followed, a sports psychologist observed her practice sessions and described her as someone who had lost all confidence in herself.

As she skated onto the ice for the final round of competition, she looked tentative and fell after attempting her first triple jump. It appeared to be a rerun of the previous round. Even the commentators seemed to be writing her obituary. Then, unexpectedly, near the end of her program, she attempted two triple jumps, and she hit both of them flawlessly. With nothing to lose, it looked like she was mustering a last all-out effort to put in a winning performance. The talent and abilities that had eluded her throughout her practice sessions and the competition had returned to her in a rush. The commentators were coming out of their skins with excitement, saying how courageous it was for her to attempt such a daring move. But the profoundness of that moment was captured on the face of Midori Ito when she landed the first of those triple jumps. It looked like she wanted to scream in triumph! The smile on her face seemed more than even she could handle. It looked like she would scream in sheer joy. Her joy was utterly and totally complete. The look on her face was priceless. She placed second in the competition, winning the silver medal, but more importantly, she had regained something that was more valuable than the gold medal. She had found the joy…again.

I imagine that's what Mary's joy was like when she recognized the risen Lord. That change from utter despair to complete joy. What a glorious moment it must have been. That joy is ours to experience and embrace as well. And it could be as easy as turning to him and recognizing who he is. Perhaps your work or busyness has disguised him so you cannot see him. Maybe selfishness has put a veil between you and the One who gave so selflessly. I encourage you to step back and truly reconsider Jesus and who he is and what he has done. Reflect on what your life would be like without his saving grace. Reflect on what he has given to you. We are truly fortunate to have such a great Savior. When you experience his grace in your life, give way to the joy in Christ as you discover it again and again.

REMEMBERING
A SEED SOWER

A farmer went out to sow his seed. As he was scattering
the seed, some fell along the path, and the birds came
and ate it up. Some fell on rocky places, where it did not
have much soil. It sprang up quickly, because the soil
was shallow. But when the sun came up, the plants were
scorched and they withered because they had no root.
Other seed fell among thorns, which grew up and choked
the plants. Still other seed fell on good soil, where it pro-
duced a crop-a hundred, sixty or thirty times what was
sown. He who has ears let him hear.

Matthew 13:3–8

I n the summer of 1989, I accompanied members of the
United in Spirit Choir when they went to Japan to sing,
to witness, and to visit and meet our church-supported
missionaries in the field. I can remember the night a group
of us sat around a simple kitchen table with Julia Motoya-
ma as she shared her testimony with us of her missionary
work in Japan. Her stories would date back before World

War II. I was fascinated and inspired by what God had accomplished through her. If I were at home, I wouldn't have heard her testimony, and I know if I had just read about it, I would have been left lacking. As Julia shared her work in the mission field of Japan, it was as if a book was being read to me, affirming God's faithfulness and provision for her life. It is an experience I will never forget. In our short time together, God revealed to my heart why I was there in Japan. Before hearing Julia, I felt a little confused as to why I was in a foreign place, singing and speaking words people couldn't understand. But after that night, the mission tour took on new significance for me. I could feel his blessings flow from previous days and in the days ahead. Praise God!

Again, in 1991, on the tour to parts of Northern California with Sojourn, Brethren, and Lila, I experienced similar feelings of searching for purpose in what I was doing far from home. Yes, we were there to share our ministry of music. Surely God had something more profound planned for us there than that. I thought I was being very realistic about myself and for the rest of us. Music and words can be very vaporous in nature. Very easily forgotten, no matter how meaningful it may have been at the time that they are sung. It is human nature. Following each performance, there was no time to dwell on what we had just done. There was always another concert to prepare for, another place to be. Still, I felt that God meant to teach me something more. And he did.

On the night of our concert at the Berkley Methodist United Church, I had an opportunity to talk story with

Bernie Kim. While most of the others had gone to get a bite to eat before the concert, we remained at the church. Bernie shared with me the story of how the seed of faith was first planted in him and how it related to the song "Soldiers Again." While in intermediate school, Bernie became involved with a branch of the Salvation Army located in an old housing project close to the old airport. Through the witness and kindness of Major Violet Ching, Bernie's life would be changed. Bernie described their ministry of music with Major Ching on tambourine, another man playing sousaphone, and another playing a bass drum. That's how singing was led. Unorthodox, but committed. Necessity gives birth to many wonderful things. Following the service, Major Ching would cook lunch in an old cast-iron skillet. Bernie describes Major Ching as a small but tough lady who could hold her own with any of the housing boys. But through this tough exterior, the light of God shined through. The witness and kindness of Major Violet Ching planted the seeds of faith in Bernie. He was quick to admit that his life was not changed immediately. It took many years, but the seed planting did take place and allowed God's work to begin in Bernie's life and continues to this day. Bernie's testimony touched me deeply. I thought again, *If I were at home, I wouldn't have heard this.* God had not only witnessed to me though Bernie's testimony but had also touched our friendship as well. I really felt blessed. But more importantly, God had revealed to me the importance of our mission. Though we would be there a relatively short time sharing, we had the opportunity to be seed sowers for Christ. Each concert we did presented another opportunity to share his message of love, hope, and joy that passes understanding. We may not know who will be touched. But God knows, and if our faith and trust are in him, he can use us in a powerful way.

I have heard it said many times that the most powerful witness for God is our own changed lives. A quote from Charles Swindoll was repeated many times at Honolulu '91. "People don't care what you know until they know you care." We can be seed planters. You don't need to be a singer on a stage or someone with a spotlight shining down on you. Like Major Violet Ching, you just have to care enough to share your life and faith with someone. God can use each of us according to his own purposes. In your prayers, ask that God will free you so that he can use you more fully to share your life and faith and the good news with others. There are many seeds still yet to be sown.

REMEMBERING HARRY

I want to praise (know, love, serve) You, Lord, much more
than I do.
Learn to seek Your face and the knowledge of Your grace,

Excerpt from I Want to Praise You Lord *by Randy Thomas
and Sam O. Scott*

Love the Lord your God with all you heart and with all your
soul and all your strength.

Deuteronomy 6:5

The song "I Want to Praise You, Lord" brings many
wonderful memories to mind. I first heard it during
the summer of 1980 shortly after graduating from Indiana University. It is from the album *Praise Four* by Ma-
ranatha! Music. There are many memorable songs from
that recording that are now standards in many churches.
"I Love You, Lord," "In His Time," and "Jesus, What A
Wonder You Are" are some of the ones that you might

recognize. For some reason, "I Want To Praise You, Lord" never quite made it into that category. It could be because it is sort of up-tempo (by church music standards of the time) and has that soft sixteenth-note rock feel. Nonetheless, I decided to introduce it to the youth choir, and they loved it! It became a standard at all our camps and every "jam session" we had during the early eighties. The song still conjures up so many great memories of singing and fellowship with friends who have remained very close to my heart to this day. This is a song of aspiration. It is a song of progress, of wanting to draw closer to the Lord as we learn more about him and serve him. Our desire fills us with joy as we sing and lift our hands and arms to him.

I have been taught that the lifting of arms and hands to the Lord is a gesture of surrender. As we sing and praise him, we also surrender our lives to him. When you listen to this song, you realize that the recording just fades out. There is no "ending" to the song, just as there is no ending to our seeking God and praising, knowing, loving, and serving him "much more than we do."

This song is also special to me because I played it for Harry Fujihara the last time I saw him. It was at the Singspiration worship. During the time of open sharing, Harry asked me to play it because it had been going around in his head. I was a bit surprised that he knew the song, because it was a praise and worship song and up-tempo at that! What concerned Harry was the message of the song. He encouraged those who had gathered to take the words of the song to heart and to constantly desire to do more for

God. As he stood and shared, I could see the toll that the cancer and chemotherapy had taken on him. But in direct contrast was the strength and commitment behind his words. He wasn't merely telling us something we should be doing. This was something he desired deeply for himself as well. After the service, I greeted Harry and thanked him for sharing. His handshake was firm and strong. He thanked me for my part in the music ministry and shared a bit of how the music had blessed him. Then he repeated his promise to me: "I'm coming back to choir." I hugged him, and then he left.

I have come to treasure that last encounter with Harry. He was more than a man I deeply respected—he was someone I strive even now to emulate. The witness of his life in Christ is something I will always remember. Though he's gone physically, his spiritual presence remains with me. God gave the church so much in Harry that he generously shared with all of us. He personified to me how to be a man of God.

As I was leading the hymns during his memorial service, I kept looking at his daughter, Jan. I first met her when God brought me to Makiki in the early seventies. As I watched her, she sang, smiling through her tears. Jan's response summed up the feeling many of us shared. While the tears shed expressed sadness that Harry was no longer physically with us and would dearly be missed, the smile revealed the joy of the Lord. I am thankful that God shared Harry with me and that he made such an impact in my life. I am thankful that Harry is finally where he truly wants to be with no more pain, no more heartache, and no more sorrow. God is embracing Harry, welcoming him home at last. And I know that Harry is still singing "I Want To Praise You, Lord."

It's a song he could never stop singing. Neither should we.

THE LOVE THAT WILL NOT LET YOU GO

These things I have spoken unto you, that in me ye might have peace. In the world ye shall have tribulation: but be of good cheer; I have overcome the world.

John 16:33

A MOTHER'S DAY SERMON, MAY 12, 1991

We, as Christians, live the resurrected life that God has freely given us by grace. When Christ rose from the tomb, sin and death were finally defeated, and we were assured by faith, eternal life, and fellowship with God. All that Christ is and can do is available to us. However, even with this knowledge and assurance, we are still called to work out our salvation while living our lives here on earth. All problems are not erased or eradicated just because of our declaration of faith in God. Our experiences have shaped, in part, our point of view, and many would agree that life can be, more often than not, a roller-coaster ride of ups and downs, of uphill struggles and free falls into space rather than a predictable ride on a merry-go-round. It can be so frustrating at times. There's so much that remains out of our control, whether it be the thoughtless and self-centered actions of other people toward us or headlines that make the front page of the paper that affect the world's economics and influence the political stability of governments.

When you sit down and watch the evening news on television or read the evening paper, it becomes clear why we want to escape from all the problems of the world and instead want to watch or do something that will take out minds off the reality and harshness of life. We are told by Scripture that victory is ours, but we seldom appear to live in that truth and turn instead to hide our heads in the sand. Where is our confidence after we have heard all the sermons and sung all the hymns? Is there any true hope for any of us?

In the world ye shall have tribulation: but be of good cheer; I have overcome the world (John 16:33).

There was a man named George Matheson who was born in Scotland on March 27, 1842. As a young boy, he experienced only partial vision, and after entering Glasgow University, his vision failed rapidly, whereupon he became totally blind by age eighteen. It was George Matheson who wrote the text to the hymn "O Love that Wilt Not Let Me Go" as a response to a traumatic experience in life that he never fully revealed to anyone. Some think it was the occasion of his blindness. The images of "my weary head" or "flickering torch" depict a man who is tired, discouraged, and beaten by life's circumstances. The line "I trace the rainbow through the rain" gives the impression of physical vision that is blurred and failing. How was he rescued from his personal abyss?

> The Love that wilt not let me go.
> The Light that foll'west all my way.
> The Joy that seekest me through pain.
> The Cross that liftest up my head.

In the words of this hymn, George Matheson reveals the total fulfillment of a life totally committed to the will of God. Because Christ our Savior was raised from the dead, his life was now richer and fuller, brighter and fairer; his morn was tearless, and his life would be eternal. By faithfully clinging to *this* vision, George Matheson knew hope. He knew the triumph of the cross over this world and its discouragements and failures. Though physically blind, his spiritual vision was 20/20.

My mom's cancer started in her esophagus and was operated on successfully a few months before my son, Bobby, was born in 1985. But by the summer of 1987, the disease had returned and was found to have spread to the point where my mother was classified as terminal. I learned firsthand that cancer could be an insidious disease that slowly drains not only physical life but also a person's dignity. It can literally and mercilessly devour you.

Despite the fact that she was the daughter of a Christian minister, my mother knew surprisingly very little about the truth of the Christian faith. But during the last months of 1987, she began asking serious questions about faith in Christ and her salvation. This time became a period of intense searching for her. In many ways, for us, the healthy and the living, our faith has not truly been tested in the way my mother's would soon be. It would have been easy for my mother to call out to God in desperation and fear knowing of the hopelessness of her physical condition. But for my mother, it was not just a matter of knowing about Christ—she desired to know everything about him and deeply trust him in the midst of great turmoil and testing. It was because of this that her transfer of church membership to Makiki in September 1987 was so significant. Her public re-declaration of faith and membership to the church was a giant step. Still, for my mother, time was too quickly running out as the cancer continued to spread and the pain became increasingly more unbearable.

The last "good day" she had was Christmas Day 1987. I remember bringing all of Bobby's presents from our Kapahulu apartment to my dad's house in Kahala so she could watch Bobby open his presents on Christmas morning. The only other time she would come out of bed after that was on Valentine's Day weekend—two weeks before she would die—to hold my brother's son, David, born on Maui in January 1988.

Witnessing to her during this time was one of the most challenging experiences of my life. Imagine trying to reassure someone of heaven when she is writhing in earthly pain and filled with the fear of the unknown. But she was eager to know the truth. Through the compassion and witnessing of this church through people like my dad, Pastor Ogoshi, Chuck and Sue Wang, Richard and Helene Ochi, Frank and Judy Sakato, and George and Etsuko Ohashi, I believe that my mother came to a deeper understanding of God's grace. I really felt that beyond her fears of the inevitable, a deep sense of trust and peace was beginning to embrace her and all of us. We had all found and understood more deeply the hope in Christ through her struggle of faith.

As her intake of morphine increased, it became harder and harder to talk to her for extended periods of time. It was then I came up with the idea of making a tape of myself, speaking to her as if for the last time. In this way, I could confess, apologize, and resolve some of the differences we have had over the years. I always felt I had put the most strain on my parents while I was growing up. I brought her to tears many a time in the arguments and fights we had. As a result, my mother gave me the impression she was physically and emotionally weak. But in end, she shamed me with her courage as fought the cancer that was consuming her. As Paul wrote, in 1 Corinthians 1:27, "But God chose the foolish things of the world to shame the wise; God chose the weak things of the world to shame the strong."

In this final monologue to her, I centered on a verse from Psalm 126: "Those who sow in tears will reap with songs of joy." Through her tears of physical pain and fear, Christ was waiting to greet her with songs of joy. I wanted her to know that, like George Matheson, when Christ calls her, her life would be richer and fuller, brighter and fairer, her morning would be tearless, and her life would be eternal with God.

On February 27, 1988, the Honolulu Symphony held a benefit concert conducted by world-renown Seiji Ozawa, of the Boston Symphony. In my mind, this was a once-in-a-lifetime opportunity to play under one of the greatest conductors of our generation. The last time I saw my mother alive was on the evening of that concert. By that time, she was in a very weakened state and barely conscious. It seemed like she was always sleeping because of all the morphine and ravages of the cancer. Her breathing was very shallow. Lila and I sat for a while in the darkened room and then rose to leave. As we bid her good-bye, I swear that I saw her try to move to reach for us. It was as if she knew it would be the last time, and she made the supreme effort to let us know. Christ mercifully came for her early in the morning of February 28, 1988. I will always consider the playing of that concert as the last gift Mom gave to me. If she had died sooner, I would have been unable to play the concert. As she had done before, when she saw my brother's first child on Valentine's Day, she hung on long enough to give me one final gift. Thanks, Mom.

In the morning, as I looked at her lifeless body, it struck me that all that remained of her was just a mere shell of what used to be a once-vibrant and life-giving woman. There was almost nothing there. The cancer had eaten nearly all of her flesh. All that remained was literally skin and bones. There was physically nothing left of her for her here on earth. Now that she is with Christ, I know she is whole. No more tears. No more pain. No more loneliness. There are only songs of joy.

While these experiences are true and deeply personal, they alone are not the reason to hope in God. I feel they affirm hope in God rather than give reason for it. If we try to look for "something profound" or "earthshaking" to happen to make us believe, these "feelings" of faith and hope will more often be temporary and probably fade when the euphoria of whatever caused it disappears. This kind of faith is based on something that is not lasting. There is only one true and lasting reason for hope. The scriptures speak of the center of lasting faith and hope. So does our hymnal. Do you recognize these *words* that we've all sung before?

> My hope is built on nothing less
> Than Jesus' blood and righteousness
> I dare not trust the sweetest frame,
> but wholly lean on Jesus's name
> On Christ the Solid Rock I stand
> All other ground is sinking sand
> All other ground is sinking sand
> "The Solid Rock" Edward Mote

> Be still, my soul! The Lord is on your side
> Bear patiently the cross of grief or pain
> Leave to your God to order and provide

In every change he faithful will remain
Be still my soul! Your best, your heavenly Friend
Thro' thorny ways leads to a joyful end.
"Be Still My Soul" Katharina von Schlegel

Certainly God wants us to experience all the facets of a personal relationship with him: joy; repentance; deep, unspeakable emotion; thanksgiving; and good fellowship. However, all of these things should affirm God, not take his place. Nothing should replace God's sovereignty in our worship. Psalm 42:5 declares, "Put your hope in God." He is the center of our faith and hope.

I know there is hope because of my faith in Christ. When Christ rose from the tomb, he told Thomas, "Because you have seen you have believed; blessed are those who have not seen and yet have believed." John 20:29 NIV I don't want to believe in God solely because of what I have seen or experienced. I pray that my faith will be born out of who God is and what he has done. It is he who is the author of my faith and has planted that faith in my heart.

There is a hope born of God that reaches far beyond any problem you or I may be experiencing right now. And God has really been challenging me to live these words that he told Thomas. Life, with my schedule, conflicts, and expectations, has definitely not been easy as of late, and it's too easy to become distracted from the Truth of his promise—I am blessed though I have not seen yet believe. In Christ's life, death on the cross, and resurrection, I believe in my heart that he has done what he said he would do. He has truly overcome the world. And because of this fact, Christ *is* the love that will not let me (or you) go. He *is* the light that always guides my path (and yours). He *is* the joy that seeks me (and you) through all the challenges and pains of my life (and yours). The cross, which, in the past, was a symbol of shame, *is* now the symbol of eternal hope and reason to lift my head (and yours too!). For Jesus said, "These things I have spoken unto you, that in me ye might have peace. In the world ye shall have tribulation: but be of good cheer; I have overcome the world."

A LETTER TO DAD

When I was boy of fourteen, my father was so ignorant I could hardly stand to have the old man around. But when I got to be (forty-five), I was astonished at how much he had learned in (thirty-one) years.

Attributed to Mark Twain

My father was a doctor and his brothers were in music, as I am. I don't know if that's why, but he never complimented me to my face. He never indicated that he thought my work was worth anything. I hear from other people how proud he was of me. It was a funny kind of thing.

Randy Newman (singer, composer)

DEAR DAD,

This year I thought and thought, trying to get an inspired idea of what I could get you for Christmas. The truth is that I couldn't think of anything you'd want or anything you don't already have. Buying something—anything— for somebody just to fulfill an obligation has always run contrary to my better judgment. It's not that I'm cheap or looking to avoid the hassle of shopping. There always seemed to be something dishonest and immoral about buying a present just so you won't feel guilty. So I thought, *Why not write Dad and tell him how thankful I am for him?*

There is a quote by Harriet Beecher Stowe that goes, "The bitterest tears shed over graves are for words left unsaid and deeds left undone." When Mom was dying, there were many things I wanted to say to her. There were many things I wanted to thank her for. There were many things I wanted to apologize for. That's why I made that tape so I could say those things to her and let her know how I really felt about her. I won't see her until I get to heaven, so until then, I won't know exactly how she felt when she heard it. She was so sick and weak at the time. But along those same lines, I didn't want to wait too long with you. It seems like you've been there forever for me. So much so, I don't realize that you made seventy-seven years old this year. You've slowed down some, but sometimes it's hard to believe that you're seventy seven years old this year! That's *not* how I see you. You'll always look the same in my mind—the healthy and active guy who knows a million people, who has tuned everyone's piano, and is everyone's former band teacher.

There are several things that stand out in my mind when I think about our life together. The first time I realized what the family meant to you was on our first trip to the mainland together as a family. This was the summer after my seventh grade year. You had gone ahead of us to some kind of meeting or piano tuners convention and were staying with the Yahiros in West Covina. When the rest of the family arrived in LA, you met us at the gate, and I saw you shed tears for the first time. You quickly got yourself together and put on your clip-on shades to hide the emotion. I was surprised because I had never seen you like that. I've never talked to anyone about this, but I'll never forget it.

Another picture that sticks out in my mind comes from that same trip. It's one of you carrying me piggyback in Seattle after I had gashed my leg up pretty badly at Crater Lake National Park. I must have been kinda heavy, since that was the summer between my seventh and eighth grade years. I can't imagine carrying my son, Bobby, like that. He's too heavy. But you did that for me.

I also remember when you took the Kalani Band to the Macy's Thanksgiving Parade. I remember watching the parade at Uncle Yoneo's house with Susie and remember feeling very proud when Ed McMahon announced your name over national TV. People kept coming up to me for weeks after that, saying that they saw you and the band on TV. I found myself really feeling good about that. I remember that suddenly there was difference in the way people referred to me. People used to say to me, "You're Ben Kuraya's son," which made me the center of their attention. But now, I was hearing, "Ben Kuraya is your father," which seemed to center on you more. It's just a matter of semantics, I know, but it made a profound difference in me.

The most meaningful time spent observing you came during the time when Mom was dying of cancer. I'll always admire how you hung in there with her and did the most menial and basic things for her when she couldn't get out of bed. God promises, in Deuteronomy 31:6, "Be strong and courageous. Do not be afraid or terrified because of them, for the LORD your God goes with you; he will never leave you nor forsake you." That's how you were with Mom. When Mom needed you for literally anything, you were there to do it without complaining. I had no way of knowing then, but it must have been an exhausting time for you physically and emotionally. I literally saw your hair turn gray during that time. That example of commitment and fulfillment of the marriage vows will live with me forever and is something I want to emulate and teach to Bobby. My respect for you grew by leaps and bounds and helped me realize what a special man you are.

I know we haven't nurtured a really close father-son relationship (and I wasn't expecting to reap what I hadn't sown), but our trip to Mount Hermon was a chance to do something with you at a place that has nurtured my faith and ministry at Makiki. Mount Hermon has become like a spiritual haven where I've learned so much and met many people that have encouraged me and crystallized my vision for the choir and music ministry at Makiki. To have you there with me meant that I was sharing with you a very special part of my life. Having a copy of the conference photo is proof that we were there together. I was especially thankful that you got to meet Phil Robb, who has become a special friend to me at Mount Hermon. During the evenings, I was surprised that we had that much to talk about, especially at bedtime. I'll remember everything, from squabbling about the money to almost being forgotten by the van pick up to how good the miso soup at the airport tasted, when I think about that special time that we were able to spend with each other. I don't know about you, but I had a good time.

The way you hung in with your cousin, Itaka, also won my admiration. Here was a man that was literally dying alone. Your commitment to him and his son, Conrad, was superhuman. I can only imagine what cleaning up his apartment and putting all his stuff in storage was like. In talking with Sue and Russell, I was able to get some picture of what was going on. At the funeral, I made sure to thank Shoji for helping you. He was quick to give you most of the credit. I know that the daily visits, as well as taking Conrad's daughter and ex-wife around, really must have been hard. But when I saw you at the funeral taking charge and following through to the end, I really respected that. It was not unlike the kind of commitment I saw during Mom's illness. Not that I ever doubted it, but it proved that your commitment and determination for the family was no fluke. Jesus said, in Matthew 25:35–40,

> "For I was hungry and you gave me something to eat, I was thirsty and you gave me something to drink, I was a stranger and you invited me in, I needed clothes and you clothed me, I was sick and you looked after me, I was in prison and you came to visit me." Then the righteous will answer him, "Lord,

when did we see you hungry and feed you, or thirsty and give you something to drink? When did we see you a stranger and invite you in, or needing clothes and clothe you? When did we see you sick or in prison and go to visit you?" The King will reply, "I tell you the truth, whatever you did for one of the least of these brothers of mine, you did for me."

With your cousin, Itaka, I saw you living these words. I really think the Lord was honored and glorified by the time you spent with your cousin.

This brings me to those times you were there for me during all my operations and trips to Pittsburgh. Like the Randy Newman quote, you never said much to me. I would always hear from others what you were feeling. That bothered me at first, but I've come to accept that that's how you are. Lately, I've sensed an effort on both of our parts to be more open with each other.

But I wanted to really thank you for being there for Lila, Bobby, and me. You know, Bobby is the only grand-child to have any recollection of Mom. I'm glad that he's had the chance to get to know you too. I believe that these are memories that will help to shape and stabilize his life in the years to come. These recollections of your life will be passed on to Bobby as well—they are things that I really want him to know about you. Your faithfulness, your stead-fastness, your caring, and commitment to family weren't expressed in demonstrative ways but were expressed by your ministry presence. In this way, he will remember you the way I remember you—with deep love and respect.

I was able to read this letter at my dad's memorial service on January 3, 2009. I was glad to be able to share with everyone there some things that most people may not have known about my dad and the kind of man he was to me. I miss him and still think about him often.

YEHUDI MENUHIN: A SWEET MAN, A SWEET MEMORY

After taking the cup, he gave thanks and said, "Take this and divide it among you. For I tell you I will not drink again of the fruit of the vine until the kingdom of God comes." And he took bread, gave thanks and broke it, and gave it to them, saying, "This is my body given for you; do this in remembrance of me."

Luke 22:17–19

One of the greatest thrills of my life was to be able to play the bass in a concert with the Honolulu Symphony that featured Yehudi Menuhin as guest soloist and conductor. Mr. Menuhin was quite an accomplished violinist, even before he was a teenager. To say that I felt honored and privileged to be playing with a living legend would be an understatement! Though his skills and intonation on the violin had diminished over the latter part of his seventy-four years, his musicianship remained polished and ever so sensitive and masterful. The story of how our lives were connected is the story I would like to share.

At the end of my fifth grade year at Waialae Elementary School, we all took the Seashore Music Aptitude Test. Because I passed this test, I was invited to participate in a beginning violin class as a sixth grader. Though I was not particularly virtuosic on the violin, I was very fascinated by the beautiful sound this instrument could produce when played well. It wasn't long before I started paying attention to the violin being played on recordings and television. One afternoon, while playing some old records on our old phonograph out of curiosity, I started pulling out a bunch of classical seventy-eight-rpm records out of the closet. The old records were part of a collection my dad had started when he was a young man, and I don't know how long they were just sitting there.

One of the sets I pulled out was the Mendelssohn "Violin Concerto in E Minor" performed by Yehudi Menuhin and conducted by the famous French conductor Pierre Monteaux. The haunting melody of the first movement caught my ear immediately, and I listened to it over and over. I was captivated by the beautiful sound of the violin and listened in amazement to the many notes that were played with such apparent ease by Mr. Menuhin. It is to this moment in time that I can trace back my love of classical music. It was to be a major turning point in my life. I have always been thankful that my dad had those records lying around, waiting for me to discover them. And Yehudi Menuhin has always been an artist I have had fond memories of and great gratitude for because of that fateful afternoon. To this day, the Mendelssohn "Violin Concerto" remains my favorite violin piece.

In 1972, I won the Congress of Strings scholarship, which allowed me to spend eight weeks on the campus of the University of Southern California. Mr. Menuhin was one of the guest conductors. Although I did not have the opportunity to talk with him, I was so excited and thrilled to finally see him in person and to work with and hear him play.

When he came to guest conduct the Honolulu Symphony in 1990, I felt this would be my one chance to meet him and share with him how much his playing the violin had influenced my life. So I made the bold decision to go early on March 8 to the afternoon rehearsal and wait for him with that old violin concerto recording of my dad's in hand. Noticing Mr. Menuhin's arrival, I knocked on his dressing room door, and he answered and invited me in. He was very attentive and gracious as I shared with him how he had influenced and impacted my musical life. When I showed him the old seventy-eight-rpm recording, he said he remembered that recording and that it was recorded in Paris when he was a teenager. He autographed the cover of that old recording with an inscription that reads: "*To Mark Kuraya, from Paris to Honolulu, 52 years later. All the best, Yehudi Menuhin.*"

Remembrances. We each have our own. But I am reminded that Christ calls us to a deeper and more constant remembrance than fleeting earthly memories or experiences. He knows how forgetful we can be. Christ has done so much for us. Just try to remember. Remember that he loved us so much that he died an agonizing death on a cross so that our sins would be washed white as snow. He did it for you, and he did it for me. He did it while we were still sinners. He continues to do so today. We owe everything to him. We have everything because of him. He never forgets us. He never forsakes us. Let us always remember all he is and all he has done because of his great love for us. And then, humbly give thanks.

WHEN GOD RIPPED
THE SEAM OF
MY PANTS

I do not understand what I do. For what I want to do I do
not do, but what I hate, I do... For I have the desire to do
what is good, but cannot carry it out... What a wretched
man I am! Who will rescue me from this body of death?
Thanks be to God—through Jesus Christ our Lord!

Romans 7:15, 18a. 24–25

What is your definition of a hero? Or better yet, who is your definition of a hero? Heroes are hard to come by these days. From John Kennedy to Magic Johnson, heroes have been known to rise and fall. The pressures of fame that face the famous and the near famous can indeed be heavy but, in the end, not much different from the pressures and temptations you and I face every day. Ultimately, we discover that we're all pretty much the same. Just flesh and blood human beings.

It is even possible to convince oneself that we are our

own heroes. There was the story of country music legend Johnny Cash at the peak of his career. He had a number one record (*A Boy Named Sue*) and a hit TV variety show. He was riding the high road of success. Then came the occasion where he was asked to perform at a prestigious dinner where the president and other famous leaders and celebrities would be in attendance. On the first number of his set, he twisted one way and ripped a big hole in the back seam of his pants. Totally humiliated and embarrassed, he ran from the stage and up to his hotel suite. He couldn't believe this could happen to him—Johnny Cash! His wife, June Carter, eventually came in the room and just chuckled and smiled at him. Finally, Johnny asked her just what she thought was so funny about the whole situation. Her answer revealed some of the most profound words I have ever heard. She said, "Johnny, the Lord just ripped the seam of your pants." In the midst of Johnny Cash's ego and arrogance, the Lord declared his presence and expressed his love to him in his own unique and loving way.

God has humbled me on many occasions with his unique and loving ways, and I'd like to share such a time with you.

It was when my son, Bobby, was just in kindergarten. He had to go through a tonsillectomy and the removal of his adenoids because they were causing severe blockages to his breathing, especially when he was asleep. Prior to the decision to have surgery, a number of medications had been prescribed and tried, but nothing seemed to give lasting relief. Instead, he experienced hyperactivity and decreased appetite. The operation required that he be put under general anesthesia, which always puts the patient, especially a child, at risk. I must add here that the staff at Kapiolani Children's Hospital was great. They did everything they could to reassure Bobby, Lila, and me that everything was in order. They allowed me to accompany Bobby to the operating room, and he sat in my lap while the gas was administered to him. When he was unconscious, he was placed on the operating table, and I left the room.

During that short walk back to join Lila, the flood of emotion that accompanied my vision of the worst-case scenario just hit me like a whack upside the head. For the past few weeks, I had been dwelling on the thought, *What if something went wrong and we lost him? How would I feel? What would I say when I faced God and confronted him about it? Where is my trust and faith in him and who he is? Can I ever come to an acceptance of his will in this situation of uncertainty and risk surrounding my son's surgery?*

What I didn't realize as I asked these questions was that that God was asking me a more important question: "Mark, do you love me?" When push came to shove, I began to realize that I was not as faithful as I had always thought of myself to be. He was telling me again to seek him first and not to worry. My love for Bobby had allowed me to become a slave to fear and worry. God revealed to me that I was not the super faithful person/music minister and humbled me in my fear and worry by lovingly "ripping the seam of my pants."

As we sat in the cafeteria, waiting for the surgery to be

completed, I was having a hard time keeping it together emotionally. Thank God for two dear friends who came down to keep Lila and me company and talk to us. I found myself thinking clearer and becoming more rational about the entire experience. Like the paralyzed man who had no way to see Christ unless he was lifted by his friends through a hole in the roof, these friends lifted me, paralyzed with fear, and through their ministering helped me re-experience the love and care of Christ.

Bobby made it through the surgery just fine and is breathing so much better as a result. I feel ashamed at my lack of faith. But the experience taught me that I should strive to love God more and, as a result, become more trusting and faithful in all situations. God showed me his strength in my weakness and blessed me with friends to help encourage me in my time of weakness. Like in all the times before, he never abandoned me, even when I couldn't or wouldn't turn to him. He just drew closer to me. Praise to the Lord who continues to love me, even when I am unlovable.

> O Light that followest all my way
> I yield my flickering torch to Thee
> My heart restores its borrowed ray
> That in Thy sunshine's blaze its day
> May brighter, fairer be
> *O Love That Will Not Let Me Go*,
> George Matheson

MR. WARD

A poor, yet wise lad is better than an old and foolish king
who no longer knows how to receive instruction.

Ecclesiastes 4:13

On Sunday, February 20, 1994, Herbert Ward died of an apparent heart attack. Herb was "Mr. Ward" to me for many years. And even when he later insisted I call that him Herb, inside I was still calling him "Mr. Ward." That's because Mr. Ward was my first bass teacher. As a bass player, he was my single most important influence. It was he who first defined for me what a bass was supposed to sound like when it was played. It was he who first sparked my imagination as to what was possible on the bass. It was he who first encouraged me and let me know that I was someone special as a bass player.

When I first met Mr. Ward, he had just begun as principal bassist with the Honolulu Symphony under Maestro LaMarchina. He was a tall and imposing man yet positive and jovial when I met him for the first time as an impressionable ninth grader. His handshake was so firm it felt as if he could crush the bones in my hand without even trying. His smile lit up his face, and his laughter was positively joyous. I studied the bass under him through high school and as an undergraduate at the University of Hawaii. What he shared and taught me about the instrument that I came to love playing opened my mind and taught me that there is no one "right" way to play. He shared that I should keep my mind open to many options and use the techniques that work for a specific situation.

It was in the early days of our student/teacher relationship that, after one of my lessons, my father asked him point blank (in front of me, no less) if he felt I had any musical talent and if bass lessons for me were worth the money. Herb answered with a resounding, "Yes! By all means! This boy has talent!" That was enough for my dad. He never questioned the worth of my lessons again. When I was a senior in high school, I played as a youth soloist with the Honolulu Symphony. I saw Herb offstage beaming with pride. It meant a lot to me to know that he was so proud of me. Those early years with Herb were so important in developing not only my technique and skills but also my philosophy of what it meant to be a musician and a bassist. My lifelong love of music and the bass began from those early years. I spent many days at his house, just talking and just being with him. He was my mentor and hero in every sense of the word.

But as the years wore on, they took their toll on Herb. I began hearing stories and rumors about how his playing was slipping. I experienced it firsthand for myself when I came home from Indiana University in 1980 after completing my master's in music performance. I began with the Honolulu Symphony in the fall, and it became apparent to me that Herb was not doing well. He had developed an ongoing feud with then new conductor Donald Johanos. This feud gave birth to a deep hate in Herb that began to consume him. He began to drink heavily. It was a familiar sight to see him in his car after rehearsals bombed out his mind. Johanos wanted his job, and instead of responding to the challenge, Herb retreated. Instead of bettering himself, which I felt he had the ability to do, Herb surrendered to his fears of not being able to live up to his potential.

Herb became increasingly insecure as his playing "went south." When he received his pink slip from Johanos, Herb desperately tried to get sympathy from the bass section, as well as from the musicians union. He approached each of us in the section and asked us to write a letter to Johanos and describe what a great job he was doing and what a great player he was. I was torn. I sincerely wanted to help him, but what I really wanted was for him to help himself. Ethically, I couldn't bring myself to write the letter he wanted. He responded by spreading rumors about my playing. I began hearing things about the mistakes in the section and that they were mainly my fault. I was the one playing out of tune. I was the one coming in early on entrances. I am convinced that those rumors influenced Johanos negatively and severely hurt my chances of getting a full-time position with the orchestra. Herb seemed to have convinced himself that I was out to make him look bad and to take his job. He could never have been more totally wrong. I would never challenge him for any job after all he had done to help me. Whenever we worked on any job together, he would always sit as the principal bass, even if I were told that I would sit as principal. I always gave in out of respect for him. But things were never the same between us.

It soon became apparent that Herb was not the sort of guy that I could talk to in a rational manner. In our conversations, he always felt that I was the student and he was the teacher. I remember when Yoshimi Taketa (former associate conductor of the symphony) returned to Hawaii to guest conduct the orchestra. After the concert, Aaron Mahi (now bandmaster of the Royal Hawaiian Band and former Herb Ward student) and I were invited to attend a reception for Maestro Taketa at the home of piano teacher Ellen Masaki. Aaron and I got there just as the party was breaking up. Herb was already noticeably drunk. We greeted Herb, and Ellen Masaki came over and remarked to Herb how proud he must be that two of his students were now playing for the orchestra. Herb laughed and grabbed both of us in quasi-headlocks and said, "Yeah, but I can still play rings around them! Right?" We were in no position to disagree. This was always the way he would see Aaron and me. We would always be his students, and we would always have to give him the respect he thought was due to him. After Herb left the orchestra, I rarely saw him. The close relationship we had experienced when we were younger was gone and never to be regained.

When I look back at my early years with Herb, there are life lessons that I have learned. I see how important it is to be nurturing and encouraging to others. It is not enough to just think it. Voicing your encouragement can make all the difference in the world. It did for me. Reflecting on my later years with him, I am filled with sadness, because I see a man that I don't want to become. When faced with the changes in his life, Herb tried to rest on his laurels, but laurels are never strong enough to support us. Instead of taking on the challenges of life, he looked for an easier way, retreated, and ultimately lost.

We must not be like the foolish king mentioned in the scripture passage. Growth must continually happen. When we constantly seek to be learners and students, humility is always present. The moment we think we know it all and have done it all and seek to give that impression to others, life will start to pass us by. Psalm 26:2–3 says, "Test me, O LORD, and try me, examine my heart and my mind; for your love is ever before me, and I walk *continually* in your truth." Growth is not just for the young and inexperienced. It is important for everyone. If our being saved were God's only objective, he could strike us dead and take us to heaven as soon as we gave our hearts to Jesus Christ. But that doesn't happen. Getting to heaven is a journey, and we are told by Paul that we must run the full race for the prize. In this way, advanced age will not breed fear, bitterness, and insecurity but a desire for a deeper relationship with our Lord, Jesus Christ. In him is our rest, our strength, and our peace.

My years with Mr. Ward speaks very profoundly to me. They cause me to humbly examine myself, and I hope it encourages you to do the same. Life in this world can be hard and cruel, but be of good cheer. Jesus has overcome the world.

> I pray that out of his glorious riches he may strengthen you with power through his Spirit in your inner being, so that Christ may dwell in your hearts through faith. And I pray that you, being rooted and established in love, may have power, together with all the saints, to grasp how wide and long and high and deep the love of Christ, and to know this love that surpasses knowledge—that you may be filled to the measure of all the fullness of God.
>
> Ephesians 3:16–19

THE BROKEN ROPE

A wimpy dad? No. He chooses with courage and conviction not to cut the bonds of love. Yes, the relationship is indeed broken because of the son's ruthless act. But the father still holds out the broken end of the rope of their relationship hoping that the other end can someday... someday be joined. He is waiting for us to come back to him. This is God who always keeps the broken rope in his hand hoping someday he will be reunited with us, to retie us, hoping we will obey him and believe his words. It is never too late to come home to him.

Dan Chun, 1994

When my son, Bobby, was younger, he and I used have a lot of fun together. My wife, Lila, would often describes us as her two kids as we wrestled, taunted each other, and chased each other all around the house. But we also butted heads a lot. As his life and mind became more his own, I tried to seize the moments that could become teaching opportunities.

A point from one of Pastor Chet Terptra's sermons is forever embedded in my memory. He said that we are so concerned our children learn all kinds of things, from math to sports, that sometimes we miss that which we claim to be the center and the foundation of our very lives. We, as parents, forget to teach Jesus at home. This is our most important legacy as people of God. As much respect as I have for our Sunday school and its teachers, I know that it is my God-given responsibility to bring up Bobby in the ways of the Lord first and foremost at home. This is a heavy responsibility, because it means I have to stay on top of things and set a good example.

Pastor Greg Laurie of Harvest Christian Fellowship in Riverside, California, says, "Fathers are so important. You, Dad, are the visible link our children have to our Father in heaven. Like it or not, some of the opinions that your children will form about God will be based on what kind of Dad you are." If I expect Bobby to know the Bible, I must first hunger for God's Word. If I want Bobby to learn to worship, I must first learn to be a worshiper. If I want Bobby to be a man of prayer, I must first model a life of prayer to him. It cannot be a "do-what-I-say" situation, but "watch and do what I do." I must practice what I preach to be a man of integrity. The result in the past has been times where I have been challenged to put my relationship with Bobby on the line as I tried to teach him a biblical truth.

Now before I illustrate this, let me first share with you a part of Reverend Dan Chun's Father's Day sermon from 1994. He spoke on the parable of the Prodigal Son. The title was "The Parable of the Waiting and Embarrassed Father." He shared that the father chose to remain a father and didn't sever the relationship with his son in spite of the son's wild and selfish behavior. This is what he preached.

> "A wimpy dad? No. He chooses with courage and conviction not to cut the bonds of love. Yes, the relationship is indeed broken because of the son's ruthless act. But the father still holds out the broken end of the rope of their relationship hoping that the other end can someday...someday be joined. He is waiting for us to come back to him. This is God who always keeps the broken rope in his hand hoping someday he will be reunited with us, to retie us, hoping we will obey him and believe his words. It is never too late to come home to him."

Several weeks after that sermon was given, Bobby behaved really badly during Sunday worship service. After many, many previous warnings, I was really upset and frustrated with him. And he knew it. At home, I confronted him and really let him have it. He was already in tears when I suggested to him that we just forget church. We would take him to his auntie's house on Sundays, where he wouldn't have to worry about behaving in the worship service. He begged me for another chance, but for disciplinary effect, I repeatedly refused. He was desperate and sobbing. Then I finally gave in and said I would give him one more chance to make good. He was so relieved and thankful as we hugged each other, and I, for one, was glad it was over. Then he said something to me that caught me completely off guard. "Dad, you're just like the father holding out the broken rope, giving me another chance." My eyes welled up with tears as I realized that the Holy Spirit had been present and moving in this entire situation. A truth that Bobby had heard several weeks before had just become real to him. God had put me into a situation where I became a model for the Lord so that Bobby could understand and grasp a beautiful truth about God the Father.

This leads me to say that don't ever believe that kids can't comprehend the Truth. God speaks to them in a language that is uniquely theirs to understand, and it is our job—as parents, teachers, and friends—to communicate and teach them about the Lord through the power of the Holy Spirit. No one will ever convince me that worshiping with our kids is a waste of time. It is where the Spirit does his best work—when our hearts are open to hear and listen.

Bobby was baptized on April 27, 2003, at Ala Moana Beach by Pastor Howard Yoshida. To God be the glory!

IN THE WARMTH OF ANGELS' WINGS

The angels of the Lord encamps around those who fear him, and he delivers them.

Psalm 34:7

Two experiences stand out in my memory when going through the ordeal of my second surgery in Pittsburgh to remove a large tumor on my brain stem. The first happened on the morning of the surgery when I was taken down very early to the operating area. I was afraid and extremely anxious. *Would I be all right? Would I even remember who I was?* There were so many of those kinds of thoughts going through my mind. I remember repeating Psalm 23 to myself over and over. Lying in the pre-op room, I kept hoping that I would fall asleep before they wheeled me into surgery. I was nervous enough as it was, and seeing the operating room would only make it worse. I kept repeating to myself, "Fall asleep. Fall asleep." Then the anesthesiologist came to talk to me and calmly told me what he was going to do and tried to put me at ease. When he left, I tried to fall asleep again, but then to my surprise I found myself being wheeled into surgery. *Oh no! Not yet!* I remember being told, "Just relax, Mr. Kuraya. We're going to lift you onto the table now."

The hospital was very cold place, and I was wearing just the hospital gown, which doesn't supply much warmth at all. I remember being lifted onto the table, which felt very cold. Then, all of a sudden, I felt very warm. It was a very strange sensation. I tried to figure out why it was happening. One of the scriptures that has always given me much encouragement and comfort is Psalm 34:7 (NIV): "The angel of the LORD encamps round those who fear him, and he delivers them." I imagined the angel's wings enfolding me, holding me close, and keeping me safe. Then I remembered that people at home in Hawaii were praying at that exact time of the surgery. The prayers of God's people were holding me and wrapping around me like a blanket, keeping me warm. I can't describe to you the peace and the safety that I felt. Thanks be to God!

The second experience happened after the surgery, as I was recovering in the hospital. It was a very discouraging time. I couldn't talk. I couldn't swallow. I couldn't walk. I couldn't get out of bed. Like the psalmist, I kept on asking God, "How long, O Lord, how long?" Then I received a gift I will never forget. Into the hospital room walked my dear friends, Eric and Jane Takushi, who had made the drive all the way from Maryland (for the second time) to see me. They had originally planned to come but had told me that they couldn't when the date of my surgery was delayed. Scripture says, when Elizabeth heard Mary's greeting that the baby leaped in her womb, and Elizabeth was filled with the Holy Spirit. There was such a feeling of excitement and elation when Eric and Jane walked into the room! My heart felt like it leaped out of my chest! I told them that their visit was so crucial to my recovery in Pittsburgh. I will never forget nor begin to repay their love and encouragement. Through them, I experienced once again God's supernatural love and compassion. Praise be to God!

SPIKE

Praise be to the God the Father of our Lord Jesus Christ, who has blessed us in the heavenly realms with every spiritual blessing in Christ.

Ephesians 1:3

I n 1997, I had a tumor removed from my brain stem. By the time the tumor was diagnosed it had almost completely engulfed my entire brain stem. Many of my bodily functions had shut down. I couldn't swallow. I couldn't walk. I couldn't urinate. I was having trouble breathing. My condition was so critical that if I had waited another week, I would probably have died. Because of the complexity and delicate nature of the surgery, Dr. Taniguchi, my surgeon in Honolulu, recommended that I return to Allegheny General Hospital in Pittsburgh for the procedure. He arranged for Dr. Takanori Fukushima, one of the foremost neurosurgeons in the world, to once again perform a lifesaving procedure on me. (The first time was in 1995 when he clipped an aneurysm on the left side of brain above my ear.) I learned later that it took Dr. Fukushima twelve hours to complete what he had set out to do! I believe in my heart that God made a way for me to be seen by and operated on by someone whose gifts and skilled hands would save my life. After the surgery, I spent several days in intensive care. I was relieved when I was told I would be moved up to critical care. It encouraged my heart to know that the recovery process could begin. One of the things I would have to submit to in critical care was rehab treatment. I was unable to walk at all and had experienced so much muscle atrophy that my legs felt useless. The therapists were these young women who didn't really appear strong enough to help me, but they bent and pushed my muscles to the point that I was exhausted after each session. I believe that I only attended four sessions before they recommended me for physical therapy to prepare me for the trip home.

While in critical care, I had a roommate. I knew him only as Spike. I learned that Spike was a man in his sixties and that he had been on a ladder at his house for some reason. The ladder fell and tossed him against a water pipe in such a way that the carotid artery in his neck was severed. Somehow he was able to call an ambulance and wait in front of his house until help arrived. Surgery was done to repair the damaged artery, but apparently there was also some muscle damage that left his face slightly contorted. All of this I learned by "eavesdropping" and overhearing the conversation Lila had with his wife.

Spike was a really nice man. Since the curtain was always drawn between our beds, my main contact with what Spike was up to was to listen in on the conversations he had with his nurses, doctors, and visitors. I remember one time in particular when I heard him eating Doritos in his bed. The smell of the cheese and the sound of his crunching wafted through the curtain, and I remember feeling so jealous that he could do that. At that point, I was still being tube fed, but I'll always remember how good those Doritos smelled.

One day, I heard Spike's family gathered around him, and from the conversations, I learned that his doctor was going to come in to update them on his prognosis and options for additional surgery to repair the muscle damage in his face. But before that happened, I heard the familiar words of Scripture that accompanied the Lord's Supper being spoken by their pastor. It had been so long since I had heard those words, and I remember praying silently with them and taking the bread and the cup in my heart with them. It was a deeply emotional time for me as I had felt the Lord leaning over me to both renew and comfort me. The doctor came in soon after and reassured the family that Spike was doing well. I overheard him tell the family that because of the condition of Spike's healing artery there was risk if more surgery were to be done to his face. I remember Spike saying he didn't want to look disfigured for his daughters and grandchildren. The response of his family was immediate and strong as they assured Spike that it didn't matter what he looked like, because they loved him for the person that he was and not how he looked. I imagined them hugging and being close to him as they reassured them. That outpouring of love just caused me to sob and weep tears of joy for this man as I heard and felt all the love that was being expressed to him in his time of need. I felt privileged to have been a witness to their outpouring of unconditional love. It still warms my heart today.

Spike was discharged a short time later, and I had a chance to meet him briefly before he left. Lila had become very friendly with his wife, and the good-byes were warm and heartfelt. We learned that one of his daughters worked for one of the airlines, so it was possible that they would one day make it to Hawaii. *What a happy reunion that will be*, I thought.

About a week later, Spike came back to the hospital for a checkup with his doctor. He and his wife came down to physical therapy—where I was—and we were able to see each other once again. We encouraged them to come to Hawaii again, and just before he left, Spike leaned over to me and said, "When we get to Hawaii, we'll get together and have a nice meal." We laughed and said our good-byes. I hope Spike is doing well. God blessed him with a beautiful family. God bless you, Spike.

Even though I walk through the valley of the shadow of death, I will fear no evil, for you are with me. That was and is a promise kept. I praise and thank God for blessing my life with his touch in such a special way when I was so discouraged and unsure about the future. I am so thankful for that brief encounter with Spike and his family. It was like a gentle rain on a dry and parched desert. God ministered to me in my time of need through their presence and their lives. Thank you, Lord, for your constant care and undying love for me. I am still learning to trust and believe that you will never leave or forsake me. Thank you, Father.

DEEP WATERS

Immediately Jesus made the disciples get into the boat and go on ahead of him to the other side, while he dismissed the crowd. After he had dismissed them, he went up on a mountainside by himself to pray. When evening came, he was there alone, but the boat was already a considerable distance from land, buffeted by the waves because the wind was against it.

During the fourth watch of the night Jesus went out to them, walking on the lake. When the disciples saw him walking on the lake, they were terrified. "It's a ghost," they said, and cried out in fear.

But Jesus immediately said to them: "Take courage! It is I. Don't be afraid."

Lord, if it's you," Peter replied, "tell me to come to you on the water."

"Come," he said.

Then Peter got down out of the boat, walked on the water and came toward Jesus. But when he saw the wind, he was afraid and, beginning to sink, cried out, "Lord, save me!"

Immediately Jesus reached out his hand and caught him. "You of little faith," he said, "why did you doubt?"
Matthew 14:22–31

Reading Matthew's account of when Jesus walked on the water reminded me of a song I discovered by accident in the bookstore of the Crystal Cathedral in Garden Grove, California, titled "If I'd Had My Way" by Janet Paschal. There's a line in the chorus that goes, "If I'd had my way, I would have been wading through the river when you wanted me to walk upon the sea."

In the past, when I read this story, I would shake my head in pity at the disciples for their lack of faith and courage. After all, they had been with Jesus 24/7 for almost three years! I often wondered about the disciples' reaction until I found myself in very deep waters in October and part of November of 2009. I loudly and desperately called out to Jesus to "come," like Peter did. He came, walking on those deep waters, and bid me to come to him. I reached for him desperately and lunged for his grasp but, like Peter, sank like a lead weight. My prayer every day was, "Jesus, save me!" But instead of feeling his saving hand, I felt as if I was caught in a strong undertow and being pulled to even deeper waters. Instead of looking up and fastening my eyes on his outstretched hand, I continued to look down at the water and found myself drowning in my own desperation, discouragement, and fear.

I wish I could tell you that I was a pillar of faith and hope, but I wasn't. I wasn't necessarily praying to God. I was more crying and pleading to him to deliver me from my situation. It even degenerated to the point where I doubted if he was hearing me. "Out of the depths I cry to you, O LORD; O LORD, hear my voice. Let your ears be attentive to my cry for mercy" (Psalm 130:1, NIV). Even my favorite psalm, Psalm 23, had an addendum of doubt. "Even though I walk through the valley of the shadow of death, I will not fear, for Thou art with me" (Psalm 23:4) But where was he when I needed him? I find myself embarrassed and ashamed to admit these things to you, because he proved again and again that great is his faithfulness. My heart and my eyes were just too closed to see. But slowly his spirit started to penetrate and soften my heart. I began to read his Word again and hear his voice speaking to me once more. I was far from being cured from my affliction, but I was well on the way to being healed.

Jesus was with me all the time, just as he promised. Though I was in deep and murky waters, far from the shore, he was with me in my darkest hours, just as he was during the good times. Whether I was close or far away, he had never abandoned me.

> Where can I go from your Spirit? Where can I flee from your presence? If I go up to the heavens, you are there; if I make my bed in the depths, you are there. If I rise on the wings of the dawn, if I settle on the far side of the sea, even there your hand will guide me, your right hand will hold me fast.
>
> Psalm 139:7–10

His Word and his promises began to comfort my troubled and fear-filled heart and anxiety-filled mind once again. The many hours spent alone in the hospital were difficult, as my mind became a battlefield between my fear and doubt and God's Word. I would read the Psalms over and over and over. I returned to Psalm 42 again and again as I would read and pray, "Deep calls to deep in the roar of your waterfalls; all your waves have swept over me. By day the Lord directs his love, at night his song is with me-a prayer to the God of my life" (Psalm 42:7–8). I was also reassured by reading and rereading Jonah's prayer when he was swallowed by the fish.

> From inside the fish Jonah prayed to the LORD his God. He said: "In my distress I called to the LORD, and he answered me. From the depths of the grave I called for help, and you listened to my cry. You hurled me into the deep, into the very heart of the seas, and the currents swirled about me; all your waves and breakers swept over me… When my life was ebbing away, I remembered you, LORD, and my prayer rose to you, to your holy temple."
>
> Jonah 2:1–4, 7

Every day is a challenge to practice what Psalm 25 encourages to do: "To you, O Lord, I lift up my soul; in you I trust, O my God" (Psalm 25:1).

Daily, I am challenged to lift all that I am in sacrifice to

God. This is the only way I will be able to truly and wholly trust and hope in him and not lean on my own understanding or give in to my fears and discouragement. Some days, the burden is heavy. Other days, it is bearable. I cherish all the love and prayers I have been so fortunate to receive from people I know and from people in places that I don't know. I give all praise and glory to God. I'd like to share a reading from the Worship Bible that has encouraged and comforted me in the past and continues to do so to this day. This a letter from God, speaking to his beloved:

> I have something important for you to understand. Our relationship is based on My faithfulness. Your faith may wax and wane, but My faithfulness endures forever. I will never let you go. So put your trust in Me. In every situation, remember these words: Don't be afraid; just believe.
>
> I know the plans I have for you; plans to prosper you, not to harm you; plans to give you hope and a future. But this will only happen if you put your hope in Me and live according to My Word.
>
> Don't be afraid; just believe. That is your responsibility in our relationship: Believe that My love for you is unfailing; believe and trust in My goodness. And when you get discouraged, quickly turn to Me; call out to Me for help and I will deliver you from trouble. My

faithfulness will be your shield and your fortress. I will fill you with joy and peace as you trust in Me, so that you may overflow with hope by the power of My Spirit.

Don't be afraid; just believe. Be strong and courageous, for I am with you. I will not fail you nor forsake you, I will never betray my faithfulness. I am the Lord; when you hope in Me you will not be disappointed.

MY TESTIMONY

You have blessed me every day of my life in new and
surprising ways.
You have satisfied the deepest longings of my heart.
You have guarded and guided through every trial I've
faced.
You loved me with a love undeserved even when I would
turn away.
You led me to the place where I could finally know You
As Jesus, my Savior, Redeemer, and my Lord.

As I look back, reflect on the years,
I stand amazed at just what You have done.
You presence is sure, every promised is true.
Nothing is impossible when my heart set on You.
When I see the height and the depth and breadth of Your
great compassion:
Great is Thy faithfulness!
Great is Thy faithfulness!

You are righteous and good and worthy of trust.
You never change.

And lo, You are near, You never will leave,
Jehovah Shammah.

As I look back, reflect on the years,
I stand amazed at just what You have done.
You presence is sure, every promised is true.
Nothing is impossible when my heart set on You.
When I see the height and the depth and breadth of Your
great compassion:
Great is Thy faithfulness!
Great is Thy faithfulness!
My Testimony
Mark N. Kuraya, November 2000

The thought "God is able" has been in my mind and in my heart throughout most of the year. A day hasn't gone by when I haven't said it aloud. It customarily happens on my morning walk. I start by parking on the mall level of Ala Moana Center in front of Longs. I proceed to climb the stairs in the parking lot to the third level and continue walking in front of Hallmark, Diva, Footlocker, and the Honolulu Coffee Company. When I reach the elevator, I walk around and take the short two flights of stairs that take me down to where I am on the level just below Armani and I can look up at the Honolulu Coffee Company kiosk. I then head toward the Macy's side of the mall. I take the escalator up to the third level and walk by House of Music and Bubba Gump's and take the escalator down to the mall level once I reach Macy's. I then head west and take the stairs, which lead me down to the street level right outside Speedo. I turn left and walk in front of Iida's, Walden Books, and the side of the Center Stage in the direction of the Makai Market. I take the stairs by the Makai Market up to the mall level and proceed back in the direction of Longs. When I reach Sears, I go around the Ala Moana Boulevard side of Sears and end up right in front of Longs again and the parking lot stairs up to the third level. To do one lap takes me about twenty minutes. I do three laps Monday through Friday. On Saturday, I usually walk at Pearlridge Mall Phase One. I must confess that I'm not energetic every day. There are many days that either my muscles ache or I didn't get a good night's sleep. I know I would not complete my walk or even have the ability to walk if it weren't for the grace and mercy of God. My many exclamations of "God is able" have been a combination of exhaustion, relief, amazement, and thanksgiving.

From the very beginning, I had decided to trust God in whatever happened to me through my many health problems and challenges. I've tried really hard never to say or think, "Why me?" or "Why, Lord?" It's been my deepest desire to trust my sovereign and loving Father, even in the midst of difficulty and hardship. However, I must admit that this is not an easy thing to do when there are events that remind me that I will probably never play the bass again and perform the music I've loved all my life. When I listen to the pieces, concertos, or symphonies I have been fortunate enough to perform, my heart physically aches. There is still a deep longing and yearning for the music that was so much a part of my life.

In his senior year in high school, my son, Bobby, participated in a weeklong music workshop. At the end of the week, there was a big concert featuring the string orchestra, jazz band, concert band, and orchestra. I spent about three quarters of the concert in prayer, asking God to comfort my aching heart. As proud as I was that Bobby was playing, the music that was being performed reminded me of what may never be for me again.

Another thing that was taken away was my singing voice. Because of all the tubes that were put down my throat, as well as a tracheotomy, I lost the use of one vocal chord and about five steps off the top of my range. It now requires an incredible amount of effort to sing, because I have to push so much more air to get the voice to respond, whether speaking or singing. It's for this reason I am so thankful that I can still sing and participate in worship. Praising God only from your heart is good in theory, but it's a hard thing to settle for when you're used to praising him outwardly and loudly.

I composed the song "My Testimony" in 2000 in response to the testimony of Dr. David Jeremiah, pastor of Shadow Mountain Community Church in San Diego. In his book, *A Bend in the Road*, he shares his battle with lymphoma and his experiences and reflections while he walked through the valley of the shadow of death. At one point, when he reflects on his life, he exclaims:

God, You have blessed me every day of my life in some new and surprising way. You have satisfied the deepest longings of my soul. You have guarded me and guided me through every crisis I've faced. You blessed me with godly parents. From the very moment I was born, I was nurtured on Your Word as if it were my mother's milk. And You delivered me out of the chaos of my troubled teenage years. You watched over me through college and through seminary. You sustained me through my early days of ministry when I could have become so discouraged that I might finally have just thrown in the towel and abandoned Your work. God, as I look back over the years and see the height and depth and breadth of great compassion, I can only say that indeed, great is Your faithfulness.

To this, I can only add my amen.